Racism

BookLife

Harriet Brundle

WORLD ISSUES

WORLD
ISSUES

Book Life
King's Lynn
Norfolk PE30 4LS
©This edition was
published in 2018.
First published in 2017.

ISBN: 978-1-78637-035-8

A catalogue record for this book
is available from the British Library.

Written by:
Harriet Brundle

Edited by:
Grace Jones

Designed by:
Matt Rumbelow
Drue Rintoul

Contents

Words that look like *this* can be found in the Glossary on page 30.

Words that look like **this** are key words to remember.

What Are Discrimination *and* Prejudice?

Think about all the people you know. The list might include girls and boys, people who are old and young and people who have different religions, beliefs or skin colours. No two people are the same; however, we are all human beings with feelings.

In most countries, discrimination is against the law. *Racism* is a type of discrimination.

Discrimination happens when an individual or a group of people are treated unfairly because of their differences. Discrimination has happened throughout history. It can happen at any time and can take lots of different forms. Discrimination can be extremely upsetting for anybody who experiences it.

A person is said to be **_prejudiced_** when they have an unjustified, incorrect and often negative opinion of a person, or group of people, simply because they are from a particular religion, culture or country. A person who is prejudiced does not act on their views. If a person does act on their prejudiced views, they are then being discriminatory.

One example of discrimination is if a woman is being paid less to do the same job as a man. In this case, the woman is being discriminated against.

A prejudiced opinion is not based on fact or actual experience. A prejudiced opinion can be established in a variety of ways, but we can try to change prejudiced views through education.

What Is Racism?

Key Terms

The word **race** refers to a group of people who share similar physical characteristics, for example skin colour.

Racism is the belief that people of a particular race have different abilities and characteristics and that these cause one race to be superior to another.

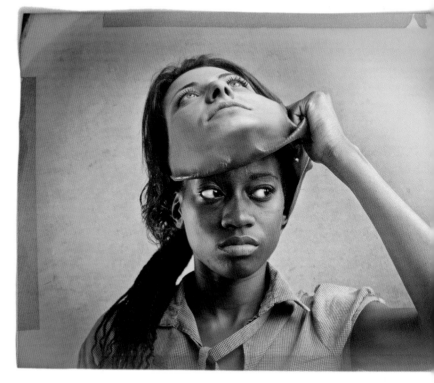

Racism happens when a person is treated unjustly or differently by another person because of their race. Somebody who demonstrates racism is being racist.

In most countries, racism is a crime. If you experience racism, or see it happening to another person, it is important to report it to a responsible adult.

Racism can also be driven by ***racial stereotypes***. A stereotype is a generalisation, or assumption, that a group of people who share similar characteristics behave in a certain way. A stereotype means that individual differences are not taken into account.

An example of a racial stereotype is that all people of the same race are intelligent.

Every person has the right to live their life free from discrimination. It is important to understand that even though others may look or act differently from you, everybody is the same inside and should be treated equally. This is called ***equality***.

Why Are People Racist?

As we grow up, our views, beliefs and even the type of language we use are established and influenced by those around us, for example our family and friends. If some members of a family hold prejudiced beliefs, these may be passed on to the younger people in the family.

This cycle continues and so prejudiced beliefs are passed on to the next **generation**.

If others around us are using racist words or expressing racist beliefs, it may seem normal or acceptable because it is what we are used to. This does not make it right; it is important to stand up to racism. Find out more about how you can do this on page 22.

People who are being racist may be doing so through a lack of education or understanding. They may be lacking in self-confidence or self-esteem. They might feel threatened by people of a different race or culture and so it makes them feel better to make others feel bad about themselves. This does not make racism acceptable; it is important to remember that nobody should be discriminated against.

This cycle can be broken through education.

In 2010 in America, it was reported that African-American people received prison sentences that were 10% longer than sentences received by white people.

How Does Racism *Happen?*

Racism can happen at any time and in any place; this includes at school, in public, at home and online.

In a survey of young people, 89% had witnessed or experienced racism. Racism most commonly happened at school or online.

43% At school

33% Online

If a person is being bullied or singled out at school because of their race, this is racism. If you experience this, or see it happening to somebody else, it is important to report it to a teacher or a responsible adult.

Cyber bullying is any form of bullying behaviour that is done online. The most common platform for cyber bullying is social media. If somebody online is using racist language, make sure you speak to a responsible adult about it.

Racism can also happen when in public and might take the form of racist language or actions. If you see a person being racially abused, tell the person looking after you straight away.

Real Life

A young Muslim girl, called Ruhi Rahman, was racially abused by a stranger whilst on a train with her sister in the city of Newcastle in England in 2015. The stranger began to shout discriminatory and racist comments. Others on the train stood up to the stranger by telling him to stop and eventually he was told to get off the train.

Between 2009 and 2010, there were over 55,000 racist incidents reported to the police in England and Wales. The figures recorded may not be accurate, however, as people who have experienced a racial attack might not always report it to the police.

How Does Racism Make Others Feel?

When a person experiences racism, they can feel lots of different emotions. These might include feeling sad, alone, angry or scared. For others, racist attacks can cause serious and long-term health issues, such as **depression**, anxiety or low self-esteem.

A person experiencing racism might feel singled out. This could make that person feel lonely or as if they do not have anybody to support them. If you know somebody who might be feeling like this, it is important to let them know that they can talk to you about what is happening.

In a study of 800 Australian children, it was discovered that when they experienced racism, they also experienced physical reactions, such as headaches, sweating and trembling.

A person who experiences racism might feel it has affected their confidence. This could make that person not want to go to school or even leave the house.

Racist views passed down from parents and grandparents might make younger people feel that they can only be friends with others who are of the same race, background or culture as them. It is important to make friends with everybody and make every person feel included.

Racism can create a community of people who do not trust each other. In its most extreme form, this can lead to race related attacks or riots.

13

Experiencing Racism

If you experience racism in any form, it is important that you report it to a responsible adult, for example a parent or a member of the authorities. If you feel you are in immediate danger, call the police.

If the person who has been racist towards you is a stranger, try to remember as many details as you can about them, for example what they look like or what they are wearing, so that you can report the incident.

If the same person or group of people are being racist towards you regularly, speak to a teacher or whoever looks after you, so they can deal with the problem. Try to keep some evidence of what has been happening, for example a diary of events, so you can show others who can help you.

Although the actions of those being racist might be upsetting or make you want to avoid situations, such as going to school, try not to let it affect your life. This may make you feel worse in the long term.

It is also important to keep safe. Rather than spending time alone when at school, stay with your friends and try not to react angrily if somebody is upsetting you. If you are upset or worried, speak to a teacher about how you are feeling.

Remember! If a person is being racist towards you, it is not your fault. Nobody deserves to be discriminated against.

Racism *and the Media*

Key Terms

The word ***media*** refers to the way information is passed to groups of people, for example via television, the internet or newspapers. A ***journalist*** gathers information and it is shown through the media.

A poll completed in 2014 found that four out of five people believe that the way the media shows British ethnic minorities promotes racism.

Everyday, people all around the world use media to find out information, for example the latest news stories. The way in which the media presents information can, therefore, often have an influence on people's opinions and feelings towards a particular situation, person or group of people.

16

One opinion is that the media presents people of ethnic minorities in a more negative way, for example, crimes committed by a person from an ethnic minority may be heavily reported, whereas a crime committed by a white person may not be. This can have an impact on people's opinions. Others disagree with this and feel the media represents everybody equally.

Real Life

During the trial of African-American sports star O.J. Simpson in 1994, Time magazine was found to have digitally darkened the colour of Simpson's face on their front cover picture. It was thought by some people at the time that this was done to **demonise** Simpson and consequently negatively influence people's opinion of him.

It's important not to let the media influence your own opinion.

Racism *and the Police*

For many years, the relationship between the police force and people of ethnic groups has been a subject of attention from governments, the media and the general public all around the world.

Some police forces have been accused of *institutional racism*. This form of racism goes beyond one individual's beliefs and instead refers to the **collective** failure of an **organisation** to offer a service that is free from discrimination.

Although crimes will often come to the attention of the police, officers also try to uncover criminal activity by searching for it. In these cases, the police decide who they believe to be suspicious and act accordingly. Over time, it has been consistently proven that police officers are more likely to stop, search or arrest a black or **Latino** person. This has caused many black and Latino communities to feel **targeted** by the police force.

Los Angeles

U.S.A.
UNITED STATES OF AMERICA

In some instances, relations between the police and those of ethnic descent have reached crisis point, resulting in angry and violent reactions, riots and **protests**.

Find out more about the Los Angeles riots on page 27.

Real Life

In 1991, Rodney King, an African American taxi driver, was involved in a high-speed car chase in the city of Los Angeles. He became internationally known after he was badly beaten by members of the Los Angeles police force. Despite video evidence of the incident, the four officers involved were **acquitted** of all charges. This incident is largely thought to have started the Los Angeles riots, which took place in 1992.

Campaigns

In 2011, the Australian Government agreed to develop their National Anti-Racism Strategy, with the aim of improving knowledge and awareness of racism and to suggest ways in which it could be prevented.

Australia

RACISM. IT STOPS WITH ME

A campaign, called "Racism. It Stops With Me." was introduced. The campaign guidelines were established with the hope of reducing the amount of racist incidents that occur by helping others to understand how to take action against racism within their community. The campaign also offers advice on how to promote anti-racist messages.

The Australian Government hope to bring people together to take action. The campaign has proved to be popular across Australia and has been supported by organisations such as Twitter and the Australian Rugby Federation.

The "Let's Kick Racism Out of Football" campaign was established to try to stop racism within international football. It was first started in 1993, in response to players and fans who wanted racist attitudes within the sport to stop. High profile players, such as Eric Cantona, who himself had experienced racism whilst playing, backed the campaign.

In 1997, "Kick it Out" became a body of people who were determined to tackle all areas of discrimination and inequality within the game itself, as well as within the wider community.

In 2013, "Kick it Out" launched an online app that allows football supporters to report any racist or discriminatory incidents that happen whilst in a football setting.

How Can We Help?

Talk to a responsible adult about racism you have experienced, whether it was first-hand or being done to somebody else. Ask them to deal with the person or people responsible.

If you see racism online, it is best to use the "report" button where possible. This will bring the post to the attention of those running the website or forum so that they can deal with the person directly.

Talk to an Adult!

Report

Stand up to racism. Explain to the person being racist why they are wrong for what they are saying or doing. This could be at school, at home or in the community. If that person reacts in a way that makes you feel worried, walk away and report it to a responsible adult.

22

We can all stand up to racism by taking positive action. Try to learn as much as possible about other people's cultures and backgrounds. This will help you to educate others around you. Talk to a responsible adult who can help you to research campaigns happening in your community in which you might want to become involved.

The website <u>dosomething.org</u> encourages young people to volunteer for different campaigns for social change, for example hosting events at school to reduce bullying. It is the largest organisation of its type. The website also includes advice and information on how to deal with racism.

Look online and find out more!

23

Case Study:
Aboriginal People

The Australian Aboriginal people are **indigenous** to Australia. They have been living in Australia for over 50,000 years.

When the Aboriginal people first arrived in the country, and for many years after, they lived all over Australia. The Aborigines were mainly **nomadic** people who moved around looking for food; however, there were some who permanently settled. They created a rich culture, had many languages and developed their own **folklore**.

Thousands of years ago, the different groups of Aboriginal people had over 250 languages. Now, there are less than 145 still known or used.

During the 18th Century people from Britain began to arrive in Australia. The British people violently claimed much of the land, forcing the Aboriginal people to flee their homes. The British people wanted the Aborigines to join their culture and learn their language. However, the Aborigines resisted and this led to **conflict**.

At this time, the attitude towards the Aboriginal people changed and they were forced out further. They were viewed as **inferior** people. The Aboriginal people still experience racial discrimination today and the community has suffered with poverty, high crime rates, **unemployment**, alcoholism and poor education.

Timeline: Racism through History

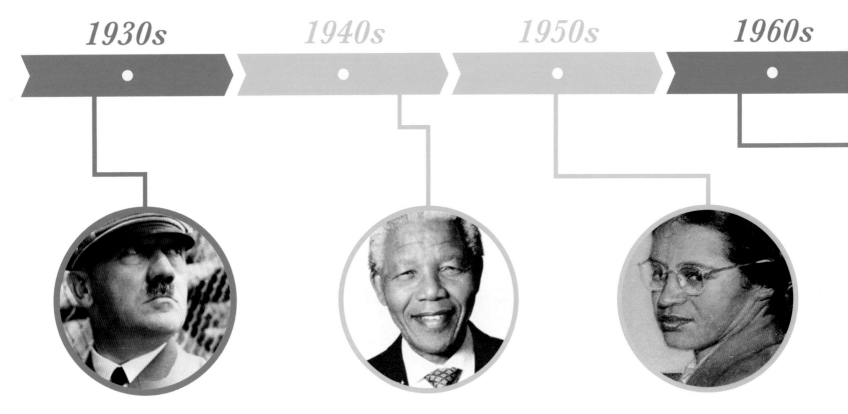

1930s   1940s   1950s   1960s

1939 - World War II began:
The Nazi party, led by Adolf Hitler, came to power in Germany in 1933. The Nazis believed they were of a superior race and that others, particularly people of Jewish faith, threatened the Aryan race. Germany began invading other countries, which eventually led to the start of World War II. During this time, the Nazi party killed millions of Jewish people.

1948 – Apartheid in South Africa was established:
Apartheid, meaning separateness, was a state of racial **segregation** in South Africa that was enforced by the country's government at the time. The rights of all people of ethnic descent were capped. The government segregated education, public services and health care, amongst other things, while offering white people superior public services. There was racial tension throughout the country for many years. Apartheid ended in 1991, helped by anti-apartheid campaigner Nelson Mandela, who later became the president of South Africa.

1955 – Rosa Parks:
Following years of racial segregation in America, Rosa Parks, an African American woman, refused to give up her seat on the bus to a white person. This act is largely thought to have begun the Civil Rights Movement, a movement that aimed to rid America of racial segregation.

1963 – Martin Luther King:
A leader in the Civil Rights
Movement, Martin Luther King
organised and led many non-violent
protests against racial segregation.
The most famous of these was the
March on Washington. 250,000
attended the march and it was here
that he made his famous "I have a
dream" speech.

1981 – Brixton Riots:
The African-Caribbean population
of Brixton, in South London, was
suffering from high unemployment
and high crime rates. Relations
between the community and the
police were becoming increasingly
tense, which eventually lead to the
uprising on the 11th of April. It is
estimated that over 5,000 people
were involved in the riot, and
hundreds of people were injured as a
result. There have been several more
riots in Brixton since.

1992 – Los Angeles Race Riots:
The riots, which started in Los
Angeles, California and later
spread into other areas of America,
began when all four police officers
who had been filmed beating
Rodney King were acquitted of
all charges. The riots lasted for six
days. Property was damaged, there
were **arson** attacks and over 2,000
people were injured. The army
were eventually called in to stop the
rioting, as local police forces could
not control the crowds of people.

Activities:
Quick Quiz

1. What is discrimination?

2. What is racism?

3. What is a stereotype?

4. What does the term "institutional racism" mean?

5. What is equality?

6. What does the word media mean?

7. Who is Rosa Parks?

8. Who made the famous "I Have a Dream …" speech at the March on Washington?

9. What incident is thought to have started the Los Angeles Race Riots?

10. What is cyber bullying?

On your own or with a friend, create a mind map which focusses on the ways in which you could help to inform others in your community about how to stop racism.

KICK IT OUT
TACKLING RACISM & DISCRIMINATION

Think about a possible campaign your class could start, just like the "Kick it Out" campaign. Yours will need an appropriate slogan and an outline of your goals.

Create an eye-catching poster for your campaign.

29

Glossary

acquitted – decided somebody is not guilty of a crime

arson – the crime of starting a fire in order to damage or destroy something

authorities – people who have the power to make decisions or give orders

collective – shared by every member of a group

conflict – active disagreement between people

demonise – to portray someone or a group of people as threatening or evil

depression – a state of feeling extremely unhappy

ethnic minorities – groups of people of the same race or culture, living in a place where the majority of other people are of a different race or culture

folklore – the traditional culture of a group of people

generalisation – something that is said to be true in all cases, but is actually only true in some cases

generation – people living at around the same time within a group or family

indigenous – when something or someone is an original inhabitant of a place

inferior – not as good as something or someone else

latino – a person of Latin American origin

nomadic – not living in one permanent place

organisation – a group of people who work together for a shared purpose

physical – relating to the body

protests – occasions where people show they disagree with something said or done by a person or group

riots – a noisy, violent and uncontrolled public reaction

segregation – to keep one group of people apart from another group

slogan – a catch phrase

superior – better than others

targeted – when something is directed at a particular group or person

unemployment – not having a job

Index

Photo Credits

WORLD
ISSUES